ELINOR McGRATH

PET DOCTOR

THE STORY OF AMERICA'S FIRST FEMALE VETERINARIAN

by Jacqueline Johnson

illustrated by Alette Straathof

beaming books

MINNEAPOLIS

From a young age, Elinor had always been interested in animals. She preferred cows to cooking, sheep to sewing, and dogs and cats to just about anything else. While the young women her age were getting married and having children, or finding jobs as teachers or seamstresses, Elinor dreamed of something different. She wanted to be a veterinarian.

Elinor had never heard of any female veterinarians. Her friends and family said, "Women can't be vets!" That job was too rough, too dirty, and too gory. But Elinor stood firm.

I can do this! It was 1907. Times were changing. Every year more women were graduating from medical school. Why couldn't she be an animal doctor?

So Elinor sent out applications, one after another, to veterinary schools across the country.

And one after another, the replies all came back with the same answer:
No.

All except one.

Elinor's skirt swished as she entered the lecture hall for the start of the new school year at Chicago Veterinary College. All eyes turned her way. She tried to ignore the hushed whispers. Straightening her back, Elinor held her head high as she took her seat.

Soon the new students were ready to begin.
One hundred and thirty-seven men . . .
and Elinor.

Elinor soon realized that getting accepted to veterinary school wasn't going to be the hardest part. Her male classmates made it clear that she was not welcome, saying:

"Women are not smart enough."

"Women are not strong enough."

"Go back to the kitchen."

Their comments stuck in her head. Maybe they were right.

What if she *wasn't* strong enough to handle the large cows and horses?

What if she *couldn't* pass her exams?

Elinor grew so disheartened that she went to the head of the school, Dean Baker. She offered to leave the college so she wouldn't be a disruption. The dean had only one reply:

"Well, you'd better not, because you'll make a better veterinarian than any of them."

Elinor rolled up her sleeves. *The dean is right*, she thought. *I can do this!*

She *was* smart enough.

She *was* strong enough.

And as for going back to the kitchen? She had other plans.

Elinor studied hard, passing her exams with ease. When it came to working with large animals, she proved she didn't need to be as strong as a man. She had a natural way with animals, and they responded to her gentle touch. The more Elinor succeeded, the less her classmates commented.

Three years later, Elinor graduated with the rest of her class, beaming with pride as she accepted her diploma.

She had done it!

But when the new issue of the *American Veterinary Review* came out, it read:

The Chicago Veterinary College closed its twenty-seventh session on the evening of April 5, 1910. One hundred and thirty-seven young men received their diplomas.

She flipped angrily through the pages, searching. There, in the back of the publication, printed in very small type, was the line:

Miss Eleanor McGrath, class of 1910, was the first lady to receive the degree at Chicago Veterinary College.

Elinor snapped the book shut. They hadn't even spelled her name right! Getting accepted into veterinary school wasn't enough. Performing well in her classes wasn't enough. Even graduating wasn't enough. They still didn't view her as their equal. Well, then she was just going to have to do more.

I can do this.

Elinor's classes had focused primarily on livestock and horses because those were the animals that most veterinarians treated at the time. But those weren't the animals she saw when she walked down the streets. Automobiles were gradually replacing horse-drawn carriages, and there were more people walking pet dogs.

Elinor realized that accepting women as veterinarians
wasn't the only change the profession needed.

She searched until she finally found the perfect
building. She set up exam rooms and areas to
house her patients. Then she put advertisements
into the local newspaper:

MISS ELINOR McGRATH
⊶ VETERINARIAN ⊷

Specialist in diseases of dogs and cats;
refuge for stray animals; dogs and cats boarded.

The pets of Chicago now had their very own doctor! While her colleagues may have had little faith in the abilities of a female veterinarian, the residents of Chicago felt differently. Miss Elinor McGrath's Cat and Dog Hospital quickly became a great success. People flocked to see her, bringing along not just dogs and cats but also birds, rabbits, and even monkeys! Elinor became well known for her compassion for the city's pets, even putting up a Christmas tree every year, decorated with presents for her patients.

Over the next few years, word continued to spread about Elinor McGrath, the pet doctor. Other veterinarians began to take notice, including a young man named Charles, who showed up at the clinic one day.

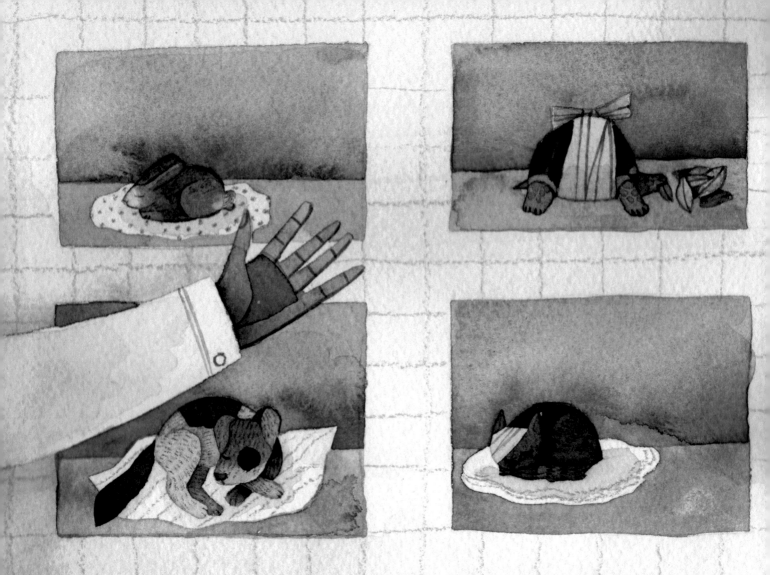

"I'm graduating soon from the veterinary school, and people there keep talking about you and your clinic. I was hoping maybe you could give me some pointers."

Elinor smiled. "Come on in. I'll show you around."

Elinor invited Charles to come spend time at the clinic, and over the next few weeks she instructed him on the treatment of dogs and cats. Soon after, they decided to get married.

On the day of their wedding, a parade of 300
veterinary students escorted Charles from the college,
through the streets of Chicago, to Elinor's clinic.
According to the newspapers, they brought with them
"enough animals to stock a two-ring circus."

As Elinor stepped out of the clinic to greet them, the assembled crowd erupted in noise. Cheering, clapping, barking, bleating, and oinking filled the air. She smiled at all the animals she loved so much and at all the veterinarians who now accepted her as one of their own.

Elinor had always known she was right—women *could* be amazing veterinarians. And she had proven it to the world.

Elinor was the first female veterinary practice owner
in the United States, but she didn't stop there. When
her own beloved bulldog passed away and Chicago's laws
prevented burying animals within the city limits, Elinor
purchased land and founded the city's first pet cemetery.
She was featured in the 1933 World's Fair and became the
first female member of the American Veterinary Medical
Association. In 1947, she became a founding member
of a new organization, the Women's Veterinary Medical
Association. She was also the first veterinarian in the world
to perform a tonsillectomy (the removal of tonsils) on a dog.

Elinor practiced veterinary medicine for thirty-seven years, and while she was not technically the first female graduate from veterinary school, she is widely considered the first *practicing* female veterinarian in the United States. When asked about her experiences, she said, "The only rule I made was that if I had a goal to reach, I overcame the obstacles involved."

But change takes time, and for many decades, very few women were accepted to veterinary school. Thanks to Elinor and other pioneering women vets around the world, today's graduating classes now look very different. Women make up over three-quarters of veterinary students, and 75 percent of practicing vets work primarily with companion animals like dogs and cats.

MIGNON NICHOLSON

Mignon Nicholson graduated from McKillip Veterinary College in Chicago in 1903, making her the first female graduate from a veterinary school in the United States. Unfortunately, almost nothing is known about her time after graduation.

FLORENCE KIMBALL

Florence Kimball was born to a wealthy family in Massachusetts and attended private schools in France, Germany, and Belgium before going to veterinary school. She graduated from New York State Veterinary College in May 1910, the same year as Elinor. The attitude of her twenty-two male classmates toward her was very different from that of Elinor's peers: "Miss Kimball has won our hearty admiration by the ease and dignity with which she filled her place as our only (female) representative in the Veterinary College."

Florence practiced for about five years before leaving the profession to acquire a degree in nursing.

BELLE BRUCE REID

Belle Bruce Reid, of Australia, was the first known practicing female veterinarian in the world. She was one of five students who sat for the final exams at Melbourne Veterinary College in 1906—and the only one to pass! She started a private practice and worked until she retired in 1923.

ALEEN CUST

Aleen Cust, of Ireland, was the first woman to attend veterinary school, completing her studies at William Williams's New Veterinary College in Edinburgh in 1897. However, she was denied permission to sit for the final exam, and so was not admitted to the Royal College of Veterinary Surgeons. The RCVS eventually recognized her, but not until 1922, when new laws were passed allowing women to join professions like veterinary medicine.

ALFREDA WEBB AND JANE HINTON

In 1949, Alfreda Webb and Jane Hinton graduated together from the Tuskegee Institute (now University) School of Veterinary Medicine, becoming the first Black women to join the veterinary field. Dr. Webb then remained at Tuskegee, where she taught anatomy. Dr. Hinton went on to work at Harvard University, where she was instrumental in the development of the Mueller-Hinton agar, a growth medium for bacteria which has since become the gold standard for antibiotic testing.

ETHEL CONNELLY

Ethel Connelly grew up on a cattle ranch on the Blackfeet Indian Reservation in Montana. "We had the constant fear of disease wiping out our livelihood. . . . I saw being a veterinarian as something I could do in my community that would give back." In 1989, Ethel graduated from Colorado State University, becoming the first recorded Native American woman to receive a veterinary degree.

JACQUELINE JOHNSON

received a BS in Wildlife Biology before going on to become a small-animal veterinarian. She is the author of *The Doggy Doctor and the Upset Tummy*.

ALETTE STRAATHOF

was born and raised in a small town in The Netherlands. She received a BFA in illustration and minored in gamification from the Willem de Kooning Academy in 2016. Alette works exclusively as a freelance illustrator and lives in Paris, France.

For all the women who proved we were never too dainty to roll up our sleeves, pull on a glove, and walk up to the wrong end of a cow. And especially those DVMoms who proved we could even do it with a baby strapped to our backs. Love you guys. —JJ

For Meg, Mel, and Vaz. —AS

29 28 27 26 25 24   3 4 5 6 7 8 9

Hardcover ISBN: 978-1-5064-9203-2
eBook ISBN: 978-1-5064-9204-9

Library of Congress Cataloging-in-Publication Data

Names: Johnson, Jacqueline (Veterinarian), author. | Straathof, Alette,
  illustrator.
Title: Elinor McGrath, pet doctor : the story of America's first female
  veterinarian / by Jacqueline Johnson ; illustrated by Alette Straathof.
Description: Minneapolis, MN : Beaming Books, [2024] | Audience: Ages 5-8 |
  Summary: "When Elinor McGrath decided she wanted to be a veterinarian,
  the world told her no, but she was determined to prove that accepting
  women wasn't the only change the profession needed"-- Provided by
  publisher.
Identifiers: LCCN 2023006334 (print) | LCCN 2023006335 (ebook) | ISBN
  9781506492032 (hardcover) | ISBN 9781506492049 (ebook)
Subjects: LCSH: McGrath, Elinor--Juvenile literature. |
  Veterinarians--United States--Juvenile literature. | Women
  veterinarians--United States--Juvenile literature.
Classification: LCC SF613.M376 J64 2024 (print) | LCC SF613.M376 (ebook)
  | DDC 636.089082--dc23/eng/20230711
LC record available at https://lccn.loc.gov/2023006334
LC ebook record available at https://lccn.loc.gov/2023006335

Beaming Books
PO Box 1209
Minneapolis, MN 55440-1209
Beamingbooks.com